JUST AFTER MIDNIGHT

Judith Kazantzis

Just After Midnight

Poems 1997–2003

ENITHARMON PRESS

First published in 2004
by the Enitharmon Press
26B Caversham Road
London NW5 2DU

www.enitharmon.co.uk

Distributed in the UK by
Central Books
99 Wallis Road
London E9 5LN

Distributed in the USA and Canada
by Dufour Editions Inc.
PO Box 7, Chester Springs
PA 19425, USA

ISBN 1 904634 02 8

British Library Cataloguing-in-Publication Data.
A catalogue record for this book is available
from the British Library.

Typeset in Bembo by Servis Filmsetting Ltd, Manchester
and printed in England by
Antony Rowe Ltd

CONTENTS

ACKNOWLEDGEMENTS

Some of these poems first appeared in *Agenda, Ambit, Poetry London, Poetry Review, Poetry Wales, Red Pepper, Stand Magazine, Soundings Review* and *The London Magazine*. 'The Mary Stanford Disaster' was chosen for 'The Ring of Words', the Arvon International Prize Anthology (1998). 'In Cyclops' Cave' was first published as a Greville Press pamphlet and an extract appeared in *The Frogmore Papers*. 'The prince in his sleep' was first published at the end of Peter Stanford's biography of Frank Longford. 'Just after midnight' was first read in Westminster Cathedral at my mother's memorial service.

In loving memory of my parents

Frank Longford 5 December 1905 – 3 August 2001
Elizabeth Longford 30 August 1906 – 23 October 2002

I woke up one morning to find nothing beneath me. I was a tree
without roots, standing uneasy on unfamiliar ground . . . what fear!
What loneliness! Then it came to me: I belonged to the world!

Elizabeth Nuñez

EASTER 1999

for Miranda

The camellia beyond my mother's kitchen door:
a breast full of medals, all over scarlet, in the rain.

My dear one in Sarajevo tomorrow
will drive to Zagreb along hairpin roads,

Sarajevo airport closed ten days now.
Of the misery and exodus further south she can hardly speak,

she hisses over the static – or is it the static:
I hate all politicians –

I'll never vote again –
Nobody here agrees with –

In Belgrade a tyrant arms himself.
Sheaves of gladioli on a table polished as boots.

Kosovo blossoms.
Heart of mine, take care, drive slow.

BURGH WOOD IN MAY

I

The stream writes its own first letter
over and over, across white pages of wild garlic
at the bottom of a ravine
squeezed between back walls and the path

to the cabbages, the church and the
scream and din of the two roads.
Invisible deer come down at dawn
and the banks are eaten to brown earth

where my childhood wrote its own way,
patchy and torn, to the river
in the valley, where the trains
pulse away day and night just as before.

Thrushes and tits sing above every loop
of the first letter, over cloth of white,
a manuscript of the lily family,
a dipped finger of water, a sepia twirl.

2

White garlic against ghosts, against
deer broken out from new private
commercial parks round here, who've
jumped out and live off the land,

eating azaleas in back gardens,
but leaving these odorous fields alone
when they browse down
through the village suburbs at dawn.

Two of them were shot recently
and the rest scattered away, I heard,
leaving the lady gardeners to thank the gun.
As for me, foreigner, shout

praise I will like a bird when I climb down
next year, to my queen of the month,
the massed margins of the white lily
garlic, garland of the flowing letter.

To church

You wear a foxglove so lightly
    since you only have
        to open your thighs.

A bell so pink, and pinker
    and floppy as the feather
        on your Sunday hat.

To church all foxglove and fine feather
    tugging the purple bell,
        the bee on its knees.

Holiday, with calves

In the ship's heart
a constant lowing,

tenor to tenor baritone, say,
among white iron,

under fluorescent strips.
On returning to my vehicle

I didn't expect this.
One rolling its eye,

heaving its head over the other's neck.
Like a daisy chain

we are all around
in our cars and caravans

like a long metal garland.

All our Major Years

– After a lifetime together, will Norma ever leave John?

The last of England. I wonder where it went.
Into the long grass beyond the cricket green.
A suit of armour sulking in a tent.

Flag and fox and stag and rose's scent,
us Norma people asking where we've been.
The last of England. I wonder where it went.

Thousands of us without an obvious bent,
us Norma people suddenly unseen,
a suit of armour sulking in a tent.

Years ago, you shyly said it meant
teatime, and vespers, and spinsters in between.
The last of England. I wonder where it went.

What luck it is to have no temperament.
A tear, no more, down history's latrine.
A suit of armour sulking in a tent,

still waiting to be told it's heaven sent
– us Norma people, that's rather not our scene.
The last of England. I wonder where it went.
A suit of armour sulking in a tent.

MILLENNIUM IN THE VALLEY OF THE OUSE

— a sestina for Lewes

Autumn came. Along the courteous rivers
willow and alder leaves flicked to the water,
flicked on the red brick piers of bridges.
A speck of rain. People sat in their houses
with tea and television, ignoring winter
coming, or any talk of flooding.

Then autumn suddenly plotted a flooding.
Breaking out, our sidling subject rivers
hijacked high streets, lanes, stores, houses.
A morning-after sea guarded the bridges,
a forced culvert, a flank, an army of water
stamping a month of mud into the winter.

Season of mellow misery, with winter
webfoot behind. Thursday of the flooding,
sun robed the government of the rivers
after the downpours. Inside the subject houses,
our family photos, those strong bridges
to our own sources, stared at us underwater.

What I remember is the roar of water,
a swift and gruff fall through the winter
pastures in our valley, as the flooding
thrust through the hedges. Our little rivers
would often uprise, but always houses
were respected, they just shot at bridges.

Indeed our shapely town relied on bridges:
down School Hill, then across the warehoused water
to Cliffe High Street. We enjoyed our rivers.
The brewery yard was always flooding,
the kegs floating regularly in winter.
But now the river ran and ransacked houses.

The magazines in Smith's fanned out like houses
of sodden collapsed cards. Plywood bridges
climbed up to frantic attics. Over the water
rowed canaries, and tortoises in their winter
doze, and cats. And a baby born in the flooding,
who cheered us all, was Noah of the rivers.

Envoi
But what I wonder did the rivers teach the houses
after the water sank subject to the bridges,
after that infamous winter of our famous flooding?

THE MARY STANFORD DISASTER

This was the story I tried to tell you in August
and failed, that difficult white week
when the children splashed and swam
in the mouth of the Rother, in the harbour,
and I struggled down too, a lame mermaid,
and overweight, but the only grown woman
to take on the no of the quick strong current.

Who can resist a disaster, said Judy to May,
listen to this, rustling headlines worse day after day.
Voyeur, maggot, parasite, said May to Judy.
This was her special way of calling her mother silly.
But the maggot listens, as the parasite reads:

*A terrible accident struck the small fishing
community of Rye Harbour on the South Coast,
in the morning of November 15, 1928, when*

Mum, there's someone on the phone for you.
I think she said her name was Julia Pope.
She apologised, a stranger long dead, truly scary.
She's talking about these three lads, long dead,
Charlie, Bob and Alec who were three brothers
and my sons were laid out on the beach, stiff, cold,
when the sea delivered them at intervals through the day.

Then I called up to you 'why don't you swim,
it's not so hard, darling, it's lovely'
but you frowned from the quayside,
more than a frown, a private, malevolent
glare. That hard white week in August
in the mouth of the Rother, in Rye Harbour,
when the kids in the river splashed and swam.

Charlie the oldest, my own boy, was floating face down.
Mum, it's a woman crying, a Mrs Pope, PLEASE
He helped me as much as he could in those hard days.
We'd nothing, but there'd always be the fishing.
With two sons without work at home, well, we'd cope.

I didn't know how to explain the horror in August,
that white week. A summer sea mist rose up to hold
the beach in its arms. The old breakwater stumps
stuck up black, an awkward, incomprehensible
mathematical series. A small girl danced and wove
along the black baulks. They were her metronomes,
and then she ran up into the mist.

Bob was my second, silent and broad shouldered.
quiet and observing, his broad face, comfort
in heavy seas and in the teeth of a howling gale.
They ran into the water, caught him as he wavered
half lost in the blinding troughs. And yelled, Alive!
went the hissed shout. The doctor pumped at him,
but in that uproar my son's quietness departed.

I can't put you down, Julia whoever you are,
you scare me, go out the back door and lock
it behind you. Heavens, I never want to hear
of disasters any more. Caller, you talk
too loud with your howling seas and ill winds.

They say that the last son is the favourite,
his mother's favourite. I don't know. Alec
was a lovely boy, your real spun gold curls
and naughty blue eyes. He had a temper,
he'd kick me on the shins when he was three
and I'd stand him out of the room, then forget
and give him a toffee. 'Thanks ma', he'd say.

Silence fell. Your frown forbade my smile.
You stood by the river, hands on all orifices
as I emerged. Can it be? The sea sucked
at its toffee. It stuck out a hand for our Alec
in heavy seas, in the teeth of a howling gale.
He was laid in that cursed lineup, in a giant
roaring like the far howitzers of years before.

May love, switch on the kettle and see that
the door's locked, the wind's getting in its rant.
Don't answer the phone tonight, it's rough out.
Did you know all ghosts are Julia, I had an aunt,
we all had mothers. Sit with me, sweetheart.

Judy, may I call you that, though I'm dead
and you're alive, over a cup of tea, it
was all as real and is all as real as the night
of hell. But it was that morning and the
Mary Stanford rode her useless crab shell
a bit further out, till the giant laid off
and they could wade out and bring her in.

She died in 1929, the very year following;
her daughter said long after, she said,
it was of a broken heart. I walked to the sea
and looked at the old lifeboat house, marooned
and far from anywhere, in the shifting sands.
You turned from my ungainly, naked presence.
'You just can't get it, can you? Don't kid yourself.'

So what's the good? Lovie, tell her to go away.
The mist hangs like a double sheet in my mind,
It flaps slower and slower in the rain each day,
it can't dry like that, dangling heavy and hard
and sodden like a stone from the washing line.

cutting a swathe through families,
in heavy seas, in the teeth of the,
seventeen men out of this hitherto peaceful

All gone and no good to gain for the going.
A wave overturned the lifeboat the Mary Stanford
You forbade all, you forbid all others.
Without pause, out of the sky, a mist
came down like a vice on the breakwaters,
children soundlessly darted away, the mothers
clung to the stumps. I heard you howl,

'You fucking bitch, I want to kill you,
I'll never see you again as long as I live.'
There wasn't a wind, nor a wave, but the
arrival of complete silence. I found
her grave. There she lay, the poor woman,
next to her three sons, in the churchyard,
as if stone was a state of shock, permanent.

Mum, it was only a weird thing, you always find
something to worry you, you always worry.
She's rung off. And what if she rings again,
I'll talk to her, there's no hurry, it takes time.
Can't we leave things to mend themselves in the end.

They should have recalled the Mary Stanford,
but they told us that no regulation required it.
(The other ship had been saved.) So she searched
for hours, and then overturned in plain sight of all.
And I, for months, did I rave and scream?
So long ago. Do I talk out of place?
Is it always silence? A vice of silence.

Stone of mist. Does she talk out of place?
This other autumn wind hits fist to hand
off Windover Hill. So long ago.
You forbade all, you forbid everything.
River, river, water, water, remember his face.
In my ears huge waves
roar on wreckage, on error, on wishing.

SEEN ON THE PONTE VECCHIO

One day I went out shopping, and in the act
of crossing the river, I was immortalised.
Behold me crossing a holy void of fact.

I was well bred, I married and, young, I died.
Angels of indifference greeted my complaint
how on my final arrival on the other side

I was outrageously outranked by that saint
Beatrice, beloved of Dante Alighieri
I who had picked my nose, picked up a taint

or two of lust, (I liked sex), *right hand of Mary,*
greed, (and cakes), or envy (jewels), had endured
the crossing of death, painful, miserable and dreary,

then in the pure bosom of the Rose being cured
clean of scruples, foibles and human eccentricities
on high advice I accepted what was offered,

accepted as my due, (perhaps my last frailty)
the revering multitudes of scholars and great men
praising my beauty and suchlike down eternity –
I'm afraid it's irresistible to a woman!

Two for the Señora

She was mourning a ridiculous thing,
her weight; the wadding of her body, dense,

active, fifty-fiveish. The boys
who didn't look at her, I mean they were

her sons, they were eyeing
the thin-haired, thin-breasted girls,

they didn't know how their athletic eyes
like balls bounced off her vivacious

rollicking cheeks and tinted spectacles,
placed her in some classical tomb

where all male observers were only
weepy angels and deaths with scythes.

2

The thick white round lunch plates
of the old Señora's spaghetti,

her sighing, over the shuffling
forward of corsetted black flanks . . .

All her churches a hundred tonnes,
each pair of wild-armed angels

grey and white and black, rigorous
in stone but never in robe or thigh,

housekeepers to the stout dead,
those dogessimas, those great-grandmothers

of a shuffling away . . .

How shall I go home and leave him —
with his biceps and his shoulders,
his rib cages and his alizarin robes,

that red my friend the Titian fan argued
is cold. But it wrings the darkness,
it has a marriage, both civil and religious,

perhaps insane or very conventional,
with his whale-mighty waves and planets
and skies of green, brown and blue.

This is a marriage not of minds,
but of eyes upwards, his and mine,
and its children are the old stories

and they are wrinkled, old and powerful
and their great alizarin clothes
are really the colour of lagoon mud.

Always in the end, using my nail,
I will peel off the gold sky
that uplifts me — holding me up

like a child sniffing at sweets
long gone stale in the drawer —
into the Ascension, the Assumption,

the Baptism, the Resurrection.
No father slips me now
inside his enormous idea,

so falling to my knees inside a whale,
I sank down wholesale into
a cold red gullet,

into the belly of the whale,
out of which a whole family came climbing back,
foreshortening calves and back muscles,

hauling themselves higher and higher
into the primrose gold.
God climbs, Christ climbs, all spring,

all the children off his palette,
and I, full of their red and green and brown
and gold and blue stories, without agreeing.

IN CYCLOPS' CAVE

Odysseus narrator . . .

There lies a land of giants, miles from anywhere,
the Cyclopes, who neither pray

nor plough, yet own a paradise of bleating flocks.
One cursed night, caught by the tricks

of a dense fog, our blind ships crashed aground,
through unseen waves, onto an island.

At last came dawn with rosy fingertips to light
great frowning cliffs across a strait.

All day across the strait we saw the smoke of fires
and far off sheep cried out the hours.

The second dawn we rowed across, and found disaster,
we found the cave of a man monster,

a keeper of sheep, crag high and huge and ogreish
with one eye out for human flesh.

He wasn't inside but with his ewes in the meadow.
His huge cheeses loomed in shadow,

and goat kids and lambs jostled in the dark stalls
and sweet whey flooded the pails.

We stare hard at this wealth, and much impressed,
I urge we stay and meet our host.

The Odyssey, Book IX, lines 105–566. Up to line 206 I have drawn the bones of the story, since the first hundred lines are scene setters for the nightmare to come. From then on, though for form's sake the text is more concise than the usual rendering or translation, I've kept the essential details.

Just take the cheeses and then get back for the lambs,
then clear off before he comes,

is my men's one plea. And bad and worse
for them that I said no, not yes;

meaning to see what gifts I could persuade
from the giant of all he had.

So we waited, sacrificed, made a fine fire,
dined on his goods. He carried a tower

of firewood when in he came at last, and crashed
it on the floor. Terrified, we rushed

and crouched in corners while in he drove his ewes
and she-goats, penning the males outdoors.

Last, in the cave mouth for door he drops in a boulder
not twenty wagons could shudder.

In the half dark he milks his she-beasts and calls
their young to them and sets the pails,

some for cheese, some for milk for his evening meal,
and lights his fire – now he can't fail

to spot us. He booms: 'What's this hiding in my home –
strangers? Well, where're you from?

Merchants, are you? Or pirates, gifting your evil
over random seas, wherever you travel!'

At the droning voice of the monster, dungeon loud,
our deep hearts shatter inside.

But courage answers: 'We are Greeks, sailed from Troy
and Agamemnon, blown to your door

by chaotic winds. We plead for your helping hand
and gifts for the voyage, as our good friend.

Observe the rights of strangers; behind us stands
great Zeus, who has no bounds.'

'Idiot or ignorant!' he roars, 'your stinking Zeus
won't stop blood if so I choose!

. . . But where, dear sir, did you leave your ship?'
I lie of course: 'Lost in the deep . . .

Sir, we escaped, but our ship drove onto a cliff
and Poseidon split her clean in half,

the timbers were taken by the offshore wind
and nothing of her left behind.'

He says nothing, just picks up two of my crew
and dashes their brains in a bloody blur

on the floor, like killing puppies, and claws them
limb from limb and devours them

like a mountain lion eating the flesh and bones
and the guts and all, and then he drains

down gallons of milk to fill his enormous belly
and sprawls asleep, bloody and oily

among his beasts. We lifted our hands to Zeus,
crying to heaven, but we were helpless.

I felt for his liver to stab him with my sharp sword
but stopped: the monstrous door was barred

with the boulder that only our jailor could move.
Kill him and we'd all die in the cave.

So I slid back to my trembling men. Sad-hearted
in the prison dark there we waited

for rosy dawn. And then he, Cyclops, rose to milk
his ewes, shifting his great hulk

to set the young lambs to drink. But then he seized
another two of us. We watched, dazed,

while he wallowed again in flesh, blood, brains,
then went whistling to his fields and barns,

driving his flocks, but not before he'd shouldered back
that rock, grinding us into the dark,

lidding the cave mouth, as deft with the stone
as cap on a quiver. Then he was gone.

All day I mumbled revenge, and prayed to Pallas
how to pay back such foulness,

how get glory for doing it. And seeing a tree,
a huge tree club, where it lay

in the gloaming, drying out – green olive wood
as long as the mast of a twenty-oared

sea-going galley – his new cudgel there by the byres,
we rolled it out from the dark lairs

of the cave and into the last firelight, and we hewed
a fathom's length. The end we pared

to a sharp point. All that day I hardened the point
in the red embers, waiting for the giant.

Next, hiding it in the dung that littered the floor,
I had my men cast lots to choose who

with me would ram it into that great eyeball
and the lots fell on the four most able.

Now Cyclops returned, and this time, either
by a god's plan or warned, whichever,

he brought in the males. He milked the females and set
the young to feed, and reached his great

hands to tear two more of us to death, and he fed.
The moment comes. In fury unafraid,

I bring a bowl of ivy wood, full of black wine
and say to him, 'Cyclops, full of sin

and rage, this was meant for you, my guest's offering.
Drink, and know that my suffering

at your red hands will drive all others away from you.
How can a guest visit here now?'

He laps it up, delighted, and says: 'Your name, sir,
first, and then *my* gift for your pleasure,

a special guest gift, for this wine is special, well above
even the rarest wines we serve.

Rain from Heaven waters our wine, but this wine
must flow of Heaven's own

nectar and ambrosia!' Indeed three bowls fuddled
the monster's brain. So then I riddled:

'Cyclops, my name is No One. My parents chose that
name at birth. No One is what

my friends say. Cyclops, keep your word. What is
my guest gift for this courteous

reply.' He laughed. 'This, O No One, that I shall eat
you last.' And guffawing 'goodnight',

he fell back onto the dung, snoring and slobbering,
and milk and lumps of flesh ran bubbling

from his gaping mouth, his thick neck slumped over,
one drunk snore chasing another.

I urged my friends not to fear, not surrender,
and poked the beam deep in the fire.

It grew white hot, incandescent, nearly
catching alight. No shilly shally

now. I pulled it out, and now my men (some god
giving us strength) came in a crowd

and we leaned the white hot point deep into Cyclops'
eyeball and felt it quiver and collapse.

Leaning from above, I twizzled the beam round, like a man
drilling a ship's timber while turn

and turn about his mates keep whirling the drill
with the flying straps until they twirl

and sink it in. So into that eye sank the fiery stake
and around it the blood boiled dark,

the flaming ball singed the brow and the eyelid
and the roots of it crackled and fried.

Think how an iron blade when plunged by the smith
to temper it and get it tough

gives a great hiss. That's just how Cyclops' eye
hissed. He screams, horribly.

Terrified, we scuttle for safety. He pulls out
the glowing stake and blood rolls out

in streams. Throwing it away with crazed hands,
he roars hugely for his monster friends

in the next door crags. They wake, call, 'Polyphemus!'
rush up outside, shout, 'Tell us

where the thieves are! Else why disturb the night?
Surely no one dares to hurt

great Polyphemus by force or by clever wiles.'
'Yes! No One is killing me,' he hurls

back at them, 'by both force and wile!' And they:
'You're ill, friend, and that's beyond the

help of all, being willed by Zeus. Your father
Poseidon, pray for his favour,

that's all we can say, if no one is the problem.
Goodnight. And shut this bedlam.'

Fool, I laughed to myself, seeing my alias
had worked so well. But fierce

Cyclops, groaning, pushed the rock from his entrance
and sat there himself, ready to pounce

on us in flight, arms wide to catch our escape
as we ran with the trotting sheep.

Fool again, I thought, I'm not so stupid. And I racked
my brains in our peril, and looked

with all my wits for a way to outsmart him. At
last I saw how to run the gauntlet.

He had rams, big and black woolled and fleecy.
I caught them, lashed them with lacy

willow withies I stole from Cyclops' big bed
so each three ran side by side

and to each middle ram, under the thick curly
belly I tied a man in the woolly

fleece. The outer rams were his protection.
For myself I now took action.

Taking the biggest ram, the leader of the flock,
I wound both arms over his back

and clamped myself underneath, trying to press
my whole self into the glorious fleece.

Now patience. Now wait. Now we all hung on
trembling, for the blessed dawn.

At last she dipped her rosy fingers in the East
and the black rams scrambled in haste

for the fields. But the ewes stood still, bleating,
their full udders unmilked, waiting.

And Cyclops, in the doorway, after a night of torment,
fingered the sheep, sure each moment

as each stood before him on its way to graze,
he'd catch a man. But such a ruse

as riding below an animal and not upon one
was beyond the simpleton.

And last of all the big ram stepped along,
deeply fleeced and heavy hung

with me and all my schemes. Polyphemus felt at him
with both hands and called at him

softly: 'My dear old ram, why do you leave
me last, you who liked to have

first place always, first to the green grass, first
at the running streams – this morning last –

at night the one who always so briskly brings
in the flock – is it my wrongs –

the agony of your master's eye – that causes
you to lag, and even rouses

you to grieve? My eye was stolen by wicked
men, led by the great blackguard

No One, once he got me down defenceless,
stupid on wine. Answerless

you may be. Still, I tell you, that unmanly
No One won't escape. If only

you could think, and talk, old friend, and say
where No One skulks! Not far,

I reckon. I'd splatter his brains over the cave
floor to ease my own and soothe

my heart of all the suffering miserable No One
heaps on it. Well, walk on.'

When the flock had got beyond the courtyard
and its cave, I quietly untied

myself, and then my men, and drove our booty,
I mean our rich new property,

the fat, long-legged sheep, down to the sea shore,
where our mates hailed us with joy

from the ships, but then with loud sorrowing
for those murdered. But, hurrying,

frowning at them to be quiet, I had them
tumble the sheep aboard and bade them

row us out. They jumped in, quickly brought
us to sea . . . Now still in earshot

as we row, I bawl back to Polyphemus,
'Where's the weakling now, infamous

brute, whose friends you meant to store in that larder
of a cavern and then to murder,

you who'd eat your own guests! Our Father Zeus
has paid you back.' Cyclops, furious,

tears off a rock face, hurls it just ahead of the prow
of our lead ship. His vast throw

spouts such a wave, we shoot back on the surge,
washing towards the Cyclops' rage.

Nearly, we're swept on the beach, but I push off
with a long pole and we dash off

rowing furiously, labouring to the open sea
well beyond range. Still, I fancy

further nasty insults, but my men start pleading,
'Only our silence stopped him shredding

us to bits back there – you see his deft aim.
Don't do it. Enough harm

has come our way of this savage. Don't provoke
another throw, a bigger rock.'

But my anger's too great. 'Cyclops, if any
inquire who brought ignominy

upon you with your blinding, give them notice
it was Odysseus, Sacker of Cities,

whose father is Laertes, and home Ithaka.'
Cyclops groans, 'All the blacker

is my fate, for once a wise prophet, a man
called Telemos, Erymos' son,

who lived with us here, warned me Odysseus
would one day with audacious

daring rob me of my sight. But I thought
that some big handsome lout

would come along, not you, you little misery,
you feeble runt, whose derisory

wine-tasting got me drunk and then you got
my eye. Ah . . . forget all that,

old man . . . turn round, and this time I'll gather
you fine gifts and ask my father

the Earthshaker to see you home. For he will
cure me, he'll make me well.'

And I shout back, 'If only I could ensure your death
and hurl you down from this life

to Hell, as I can swear your eye will never ever
heal, whoever your so-called father!'

At this he lifts his hands to starry Heaven
and prays out loud to his raven-

haired god. 'Great Poseidon, who embraces
the earth, hear my deep curses.

If you admit me as your own, then give notice
that Laertes' son, the Sacker of Cities,

Odysseus, who lives in Ithaka, never will find
his home again. But if fate send

him home, to his own strong house, to his country,
then let him make a sorry entry,

late, having lost his friends, sent in some one
else's ship, and ill omen

squatting the hearth.' And the prayer was heard
by Poseidon, the dark-haired lord.

Then Polyphemus seized another chunk of cliff
just when finally we felt safe,

beyond his clutches; he whirled and slung it so far
it all but shaved the steering oar

of the dark ship, then fell short in the water
so that a wave washed to the outer

island and we along with it, borne in our ship.
And there, making for the sandy cape

where our friends sat grieving, waiting so long,
we beached on the sand so as to bring

off our rich flocks of sheep. These I divided
fairly among us, once we'd waded

ashore. The great black ram my crews awarded
especially to me, he who'd guarded

me so well. I sacrificed him there and then
to the dark-clouded mighty lord of man,

son of Kronos; and I gave him the burned thighs.
But my offering did not appease

great Zeus, who sat above our altars, planning
how death should come raining

on my strong fleet and on all my good followers.
In ignorance we lit our fires,

we feasted on the sand, made merry hour after hour
over wine and meat till, star by star,

came sweet night. We lay and we slept out there
till dawn dimmed star after star

and, rosy-fingered, lit the eastern sky. I bided
no longer but at once ordered

all to the benches. Away we rowed from the island
of Cyclops, that blood-soaked ground,

carrying our dead for always in our grieving minds,
glad and free to rove on the sea winds.

1999–2001

At five feet the sea from milk–white waves
turned turquoise and sang out of its head
in rolling crescendos like Chaliapin
so I swam for my glorious life.

Shrimpers were playing the second opera
beyond the spit; where the stone of ages turned
almost porous and chopped itself green
along its white veins and broke

and met world centre in locked choruses
and was betrothed, fell on its sword,
repulsed armies, gained empires, mistook
its brother and its virgin sister

in translucent and irreducible silk.
I rocked beyond, where the shrimp boats
put out their strings to dry, like harpists
taking a rest between acts.

To raft, drift out of the lanes
of history. Toiling this crossing
in my cigar box room

built in the years when Cayo Hueso
worked its little butt off for Havana
and the town full of cigar workers.

Iron-hard termite-scored Dade pine
each dawn boxes our bed
with a special gold ric-rac,

post-industrial bedroom
leafing me all day into the trees.
I sweat among shadows.

ISLAND PURSUITS

1 Key West

Just as great-browed
Olympian Zeus like halogen
flooded the high mountain
to the heavy sea

so along Petronia
this cold Sunday evening,
yet sunbeam-lit his
contemplative temples,

O Cortez goes, rings on his fingers,
white cuffs at his wrists, gold watch
and lightweight suit in violet
largely squared by pinstripe white,

and old enough to be my Daddy –
dark brown and fine and fit
to be my everlasting beau, my ample
southern porch, my capital of smiles.

O Bro Cortez –
How in twilight, half his mass
he lightly dances,
cracker-jacks past yards

of crackly Grandmas
in crumbly café rockers –
So Olympian Zeus
danced to the cities

lissom as lightning,
fat as thunder,
lighting up time,
ignoring husbands.

2 Key West by way of Ithaca

Even now I'm living with another,
  here I'm still harried by hens:
a demon or a daemon or ass perhaps,
  a rooster which brays, driving
my lover frantic. I sleep like a hen.

Husband and wife along a road scented
  by spiky thyme; black garnished
village women – his kin; he thought
  in her he'd found his Penelope.
In her he'd found his speckledy hen.

And ran it over, clucking, under the
  rented car's wheels, thwunk.
The children: Dad, Dad, you've killed
  a hen! Chant: Murderer!
Maybe a little bit proud of the old boy.

Pecked at by old ladies, he fished in his jeans
  for the agreed grumbled–over price,
thank god it hadn't been a goat, or a pig.
  You were part of the clucking, scented scene,
suitor, hidden in the bushes of Ithaca.

3 Tourist

All last night the rooster
shared out of a tarnished throat

its dislike at the hour on the moon.
The elderly tourist in her rental bed

at five a.m. stamped on her Lorazepam,
sowed blue chicken feed

round the broken fence of the property.
The fowl fixed the glowing sun

with its black eye and, open-throated,
brayed in the palm-tree

as it had done
all night long for its hen,

but by now she hardly cared, she
was pecking round the fence, grain to grain,

and fell asleep under the palm-tree,
dead to all holidays.

JUMP

There's the enemy, ninety miles away
– line in 'Strawberries and Chocolate'

To fly ninety miles to monsters,
taking a box compass from Key West,
you square a blind spot

first north, to west, to back south:
drop down tired by twilight to
there be reds making the hotel bed.

There be goat flocks, and oxen pairs
of a Siamese colour, and pirate
plumed groves of bamboo

flourishing the bends of a river in whose
bays the Royal Palms stand
like saint baptists, the masts of Cuba.

There be sweeter ways to jump
from Duval Street to the Malecon.
First on one side if you were a red balloon

you could spy on Havana's courtly pillars
brightly with your little eye,
– the slender dancers twirl in debris –

and if I was up in my red balloon
on the other side I'd wave
to the same cattle egrets, and to the malls

where there be monsters chomping.
A walled horizon of beefburgers.
No one eats a balloon.

Making love

Her lover in his half-waking throes,
threshing his arms against her naked shoulder,

smells like a baby of sleep and food, of piss
and shit and sleep, bringing the woollen

blankets and the dolls, even the worn pink
cot bars of her old nursery to lull her.

But after her babyhood who can explain these things –
she can't spend a minute more in his arms,
she must hop up, make tea, make coffee,

make toast, make the day like a cake set
to bake in the heavenly white Sears Roebuck
oven she got yesterday. Sweet day, good day.

SUNSHINE

A speed boat, a wake
like a silver-fish.

A wind like crowsfeet
treading the cloudback.

The pointed husks empty
of fronds and slowly waiting to fall off,

and sun, mad as the hatter,
eyes glinting through the blind slats

wherever my restless head twists
on the very pink pillow-slip,

that old sun gets to me.
I wrote 'she was so sweet'

while waiting – but in what
airport, what marina gifte shoppe –

for the word. That silver fish
slipped across the ocean like my kitchen floor –

I must sell up; so the word came.
O kitchen floor!

Very high up I lurched across someone else's
speedboat slewing across someone else's ocean

leaving that wake of a dolphin
of the kitchen. 'She was so sweet',

I wrote it like a mad palm-tree,
I shed, I fall off

and yes, you were, you flew to me
(I grow another, I fall off).

DIARY OF A MOVING PART

I STARTING

March 20 *Hare dancing*

A March cap of hair, small, sleek, speedy
in her mind's movement, for where else
can hares move, in their dance between the guns?

She had asked about daughters and also mothers.
I promised nothing, it was too long ago, and, surely,
a source of joy. But to my tired arteries —

Just as she asks, a shadow springs from the field,
up from its form, and takes the changing glimmer
of a shape in its stride, and hides quickly.

March 21 *Changing*

What shall I change to? What shall I do to change?
Listen, I know how you feel, quoth the phoenix,
what next frying pan onto which next fire, believe me.

Now let's get down to brass tacks, says the magician,
the Ur fellow, taking two brass headed screws
from an inner pocket and tossing them into the fire.

The audience gasps but it is of course the tape
behind the arras; we have seen him before.
Yet we love to sigh in tune with the tape, we love him.

❦

His animals bound up to us, up and away.
Too many, flaming with colours, spotted, coiled,
bristle-pelted, eyes blue and bulging, soft

in a shrine of lard, slugs bigger than dogs,
whose fat nosings shoe-shine over my feet.
You always wanted a dog, a simple dog.

A rain of animals, a morass. Only the magic
fellow can toss them into the air, onto the stage.
I always join the audience in the end.

March 23 *First step*

The movers called today and proposed cardboard
and wadding round my oven with the lilies,
the green-tiled lilies and roses everyone exclaims over.

They'll ship the oven, grey in its blanketing,
to the foreign lands, to the tropics. Now is the time
I have to start naming, as an immigrant, and

to decide on Amerika, or America. I know.
I trust I get the spelling right for the interview.
The oven of roses and lilies remains in transit.

March 26

I met Johnny on Duval Street (certainly not Stetson,
I hasten to say. My friends don't wear hats;
we are far too euphoric in the tropics

and while everything has obviously changed,
and a terrible beauty is dawn,
it's purely for pleasure, forever and ever,

and colour is merely the revolution of light
as reds regress to deep dyed blues at dusk
as the sea grows dark – the sun turns turtle . . .)

March 30 *Reverse*

  for JMB

But it wasn't time after all for that phase
of violet from purple and flame from topaz and opal.
Only, we ceded John's ashes to the ripples

where he'd lived, a sun turtle himself,
sun gatherer, polka-dotted bow-tie flaunter.
Turning back, I flew for the cold and the dark.

Flying, I comforted myself, with birds
of all species, north, into the old blank
of black on black, and then dawn again.

And Medea

Medea leaves her father.
  Why should she not leave?
    Love warms itself in a fleece

burned gold in the moon's slow list
  east over Asia, west . . .
    She sails south-west.

But I go north-east,
  setting sail in the sky
    as in the end she will fly,

her dragons taking her into the east.
  The little sons are dead.
    They ever after cry for her blood.

The sons are dead to her,
  they will not speak to Medea.
    Accusations, accusations.

So she lumbers home
  on the strength of her dragons,
    two aeroplanes, two flying ovens.

And now that memory is a fire-shirt
and a child's voice a matter of horror,
I dread the homing of sorrow,

no pieces to pick up now,
nothing more to mend, or to invite home
or to cook for, or scribble poems to,

while they are on their travels
and coming home to see her,
but they never will,

they never want to, or will.
They say she scribbles the sky with her sons,
the blood of the sun

in the evening, their words for her
if she looked. But she was
stronger than I, and a murderer.

March 31 *Flying home*

At home the hare is bruised and battered,
the huntsman lifts her by her lollipop paws,
entreating all his angry dogs for blessing.

'We can sail! We can sail!
to the howling and the growling and wonders of war.'
As the wind shifts, as the shadow springs,

as she darts into the wood, to the oak-tree
and the ash-tree and the sycamore, where
she and I were born. May she not die.

❧

Dismay, the shadow, pants and pants.
I can hear it fumbling ahead and behind.
I walk its dark water-path of sweat.

49

I've come back. I never left home,
come to my door, open the blind,
entreat you to my table, and into my bed.

There, my always love, like onyx eyes
that gaze out of water, we should have dined
forever, on very little, a long-stemmed honey-spoon.

April 6 *Exchanging*

This week we sold the terrace cottage
for an excellent price; the solicitor
and the estate agent and the buyer,

the accountant and the bank manager,
the stock-broker and the freeholder
(oh, that was me), and you my true love too,

all of us chewed, we chewed my lost
house into a million grains, carrying them over
town, like ants, to chew them all over.

❦

Madeira, Medea? quoth the phoenix,
now drunk, dragonian, circling the frensy,
And what have you done for today, m'dear?

'Only myself'. *But that's nothing,* the phoenix
twitters down. (Now, flap: it's a parrot
stuck on a rock mid-Atlantic, heading where?)

Calm-eyed still, my bronze wild man on the wall,
water of the fountain splashing in my garden,
the flowers are nursed in the garden, a short season.

April 10 *Ghosts*

What shall I change to? What shall I do to change?
The hare dashes from her form.
There thunder by the ghost devils,

devils for the ladies in their red-brandied breaths,
puffing after the girl hare,
the soul of us all, which now skulks in

the indeterminate bushes beyond the broken-down
scullery door. Oh, something will be born
from her, and she shall lay it in a manger.

❦

Let me lie low for the shape that will surely change . . .
to the fish, to the seal; or to a sparrow hawk
circling through the spheres, higher and higher.

The ghost hunt goes, or appears to, bugles
petering across a faded downland
full of spirals, burials and fossils.

This evening I hide my ghost head in shadow
in the audience of the Ur man, and my
head is slowly turning through its axis.

II BREATH

May 21

She had asked about daughters, and also mothers,
a gentle form of questioning and circular.
There was no need to remember or forget,

so that in May she comes to me again,
taut still in my own ceaseless queries
as I look to north, south, east, west.

I put down far west, where the sun
sinks his cart as often as not into fog
and the local trucks lug grass, not gold.

❧

It was a pause, and a clear breath,
the wind blew off the Atlantic
continually curving, over the stockades

of the earth's temporary end,
a bay like a round cathedral,
open to the banjo songs of the clouds

and indifferent to god.
Surprising myself, pleasing you, here
I made a bus shelter in a tea cosy.

❧

It's as if, a little sad though I was
at her absence, her plump, wise face
her black eyes, her shy moves,

she makes a visit after all, the stranger
for not being made or even
contemplated by either –

of course she has other seas,
other cliffs, on her mind. And yet
the quiet visit makes itself around me.

May 25

Or was it her? Was it cousin James,
addressing a pert robin on a step of rock?
Or you, stroking my sore bones

with, today, your strongest of hands
while we lie down and giggle
at radio jokes too bad to remember

for a single second. As light, gone, as
the flitting of weather, or the poking up
of Hades between foxglove and the pink campion.

May 27 *That part fleeing*

And yet hell's doorman, the hare's
hound, hunts on like a waif wailing
from out of the barrow on the old gorse cliff.

Calm, Karma. The airy and tall rooms
help me to breathe. The views are wide:
land of bright curves, and the baby seal

nosing round the seaweed, below Carn Les Boel.
The year in her complaint is silent
just for this week, in my fine elevation.

June 1

The sea, such a window-pane of waves
housed quietly by the unseen rocks
you could see the seals playing underwater,

playing at house wherever they twisted,
scooted, into one cove, out to another,
no walls to be seen of the garden of their journeys.

Then again space is torn from me and loaded up.
One night of long rain, a rattle of gears.
A long goods train rolling away that well-built house.

And Philemon and Baucis

What shall we do
            when we die?
What shall we change to?
What shall we do to change?

Into two trees? For a change?
            When we die?
Like two knuckle-kneed
rheumy-eyed willows?

What can we change to?
            Eyes crust over.
Mouths dry back into gums
Ashes to . . . ashes? whose buds unstick

late and last of the spring,
            spring of our death,
our winter of life, two aspens?
Our leaves make shaky love.

Gold and crimson shall lie
            at your root
dear Baucis, come autumn.
Gold shall pour at your feet

come autumn, Philemon dear love,
            Baucis my dear,
and in the spring, I-love-you
shall leap into its leaf, the voice

of robin, thrush and goldfinch,
      Philemon − Baucis,
Philemon − Baucis . . . And how shall we know
how to change when we too die?

III MOVE IT

July 10

The last days die . . .
    All through June and then
        July starts along its dog days,

emptying its own larder.
    Dawn has a snarl, though
        the hot noons doze in order

almost as if they mean to stay
    but they hardly stretch before
        barked at, Get out of there!

July 13

I hear a goods train
    the other side of the wide valley
        wandering the wooded ridge

above people and houses and cottages
    all healthy and minding their money,
        with cats and dogs and conservatories.

Only the wail of the train
    from other grasslands, other prairies,
        Come along never mind
            come along never mind

July 14

One among these flirtatious, undressing days
   threw me into Ceridwen's cauldron
      suddenly, that's to say

a real hag of a day: you stop
   the dreams with a jolt; the surgeon's
      paper-hatted face: you'd better

pack the silly days along ahead,
   though even now your garden
      pretends to make you welcome home.

July 19

Now we unfurnish at last. But can I really
flay off my own skin? Should it, can it be done,
such an agonised flaying in the garden

under the absolute stay-put injunction
of my wild Ur man and his wild outstretched
arms, and articulate upraised fingers

between which never blood but water
for five years has poured, sweet sounding,
into my own guarding and cradling palms.

❧

As for the silvery weeping pear-trees,
pearl twins set on either side of the wild man's pool,
no doubt they are sick of the sight of me,

hanging on, deferring the hand-over.
Skinless, should I pray for bark to cover my eyes
and root my bloody toes in the corner of the wall

and not move? Not move? Being splendidly changed,
I should have changed to the buyer by now.
The council are topping the lime-trees in the square.

❦

Oh no — Chekhov — pe-leeze —
That bird, that petite angel of the future,
screams out of the unwashed sky.

But your role is redemption, no? — *Bugger that*
for a laugh, or a screech.
A hurtling ball of burning feather,

it dives into the underground at Holland Park,
comes up in a seven floor walk-up near King's Cross.
There you are m'dear be grateful,

❦

that hooded jackdaw pins me by the earring.
The past marches past and this little grey loo
+ kitchen in the sky, *o crumbs me ane hame noo?*

Limey Harry's late desperate fingers: girders
of our Great Dome grate against ornate dawn.
The offices of London wink/slink into a slumping sun.

Now is the hare in her misty form,
the hare out of her skin, leaping, leaping.
Weeks since we thought of anything else but figures.

And Persephone

What have I done to change? How
          have I changed, and to what?

In a flowering field I saw heaven's court
        in hell. Ladies, listen

while I tell you how I courted hairy Hades.
        My true story. I wanted

the glory of changes and got a fate
        in spades. The field

faded and was renamed
        darkness. Another world.

So don't untie your gate
        until you lie with me and

then come back to tell the truth,
        I mean, the death.

July 21

The wild man was hanging onto the back wall
with both brown head and arms, digging in,
clamped like a threefold mussel,

till Gilbert with almost as large hands
with rocking fingers and pauses for rest
(or to respect an obstinacy, even the loyalty

we imbue to matter, till it falls to pieces;
which my own mind and matter ponders
now that I creep by inches out of the wavering shell)

. . . prised my Ur man off; the big sockets
staring through the dapply vines
as always, but then, the head laid flat, to the sky.

His face and arms came away separate,
We laid the three parts on the pond coping.
Now all's wrong with the blue sky,

the water's off – god's out of this garden.
Children laughing, down the alleys.
Better than they can, I know their summers . . .

I always heard them splashing with their summer hose . . .
as if I'd poured into this pool for years.
as if I'd grown in the wall.

July 22

The kitchen walls, the white-framed window.
My bedroom wallpaper of birds and grape clusters,
the light in the morning in the kitchen when I go down.

This week they are misting and receding,
I sit and rock in my black rocker.
It's a feint. They are solid, the walls.

Then the mist sits in the rocking chair.
It's a feint. Everything is solid;
The undressing; and no redressing.

July 27 *A hand clapped*

Two days' work: mugs, spoons and forks,
my oven of lilies and roses, the two haired mop,
the garden bench still peppered with shot

where Arthur in far childhood tested his airgun
from his bedroom window. And the house
in no time, heartless hey diddle diddle,

conjured clean as a hat without its head.
They shot pasts all day from out of the door –
easy as shooting a garden bench.

Boxed, bubble wrapped, and now thank you, go –
unseated, lightheaded, hatless,
hardly know where to go, elderly

straw. Past, future, item: paid upfront and
in store. I remember patting the warm brick
as I left, locking my own front door

on a full house; which at once rocked
and shook as I went through the gate,
and that cottage and garden and its neighbourhood

drove away from me as I from them,
and dwindled, like mist coming and receding,
or a hand clapped across the wing mirror.

IV THROUGH THE WALLS OF ENDLESS SUMMER

And Demeter

The meadow gate is closed.
    Let this old woman doze,

feet up amongst the stacking grain.
    Let winter shiver in the lane.

Let fruits not ripe grow big and ripe.
    Let the old lady smoke her pipe

and watch through half closed eyes
    and fall asleep, while she unties

the meadow gate and goes
    away. So do rainbows

come and go – while this old girl
    goes thundering round the world:

'How should I change? How change
    what lies ahead?

The house of summer trickles and runs away.
    I tied her in the sheaves.

She turned her head. Darkness untied her hair.
    Why change what lies before?

Why build another house of leaves and straw
    when she wants one of a different size.

In wind and dark and ice
    the muddy straw lies everywhere.'

July 30 *Floating*

After that I saw my old friend (doubtful hare).
She had forgotten her question about daughters
and mothers. We chatted, like beads pattering

plip, plip, off the string of a broken necklace.
Sometimes I *could* draw a bead on it,
so I tried hard to make a lively necklace of islands.

Those tender, circumnambulatory coasts
that lie behind the magician's arras.
She had hooded her dark eyes.

I know I had become that challenging point,
that parrot on a rock mid-Atlantic, yakking
from my questionable island.

What lively spots of conversations!
When I was little, I thought that islands
floated along, waving their long underweeds,

and now I was the floater, waving my weeds,
bared of my kitchen of flowers, my parlour of trees,
as bare as the head of a picture nail.

August 1 – September 2

Therefore our summer, my love, began its last hop,
its island hop. Email, fax or postcard;
but the eyes buried away beyond the ocean.

Our home trees, pear-trees, plane-trees, limes,
changed into birds of prey and flew away.
And our summer began its creeping and hopping

like nuthatches or gnatcatchers or palm warblers,
We come now to watch the moustachioed kestrels
hunt at the island's end, by the old fortress moat.

August 1 – August 6

But first that city flat – what happened there!
They took out the lift – you, dear, could walk seven floors,
I could not. So much for the first hop.

We picked up our bits, soap, toothpaste;
everything else in store, like my green oven of lilies:
goodbye to the tags of what was mine.

We took the last lift down and down:
moved a street over and to the earth's slummy
core. Fire flew out of the boiler flue

in the area and smoked the room
if we inched the window down in the heatwave.
I was in bed and stared out at a group

of businesswomen in the back garden
sitting round a cement table and talking figures.
Work stations fired green numerals

all night, once their clicking heels
had left at five. Where was I? I put
two and three together and made four.

August 14 *A greeting*

Then we prance and fly away
part move, never end

I paid the huge bill and we crept on.
We had an ocean to wait for, and time, like
a sandbag, to fill with a wrack of place.

It was her dark call, coming to a house
not mine, in Ireland, Persephone alone,
high in the plane-trees; to a mother

abroad, panting frantic in the steps of a bird
hopping to many strange shorelines
where people were castaway and died or often

were reborn according to the stupid and
stuffed phoenix who sat on my shoulder,
seeming more bird of a lame Calousa Nell

than any hint of resurrection – *Croak*!
quoth this parrot from out of its stuffing
'*all's bad that calls for a drink*'.

But even that I could not have, being older
and more crone to myself than fruity Demeter.
So it was that call, on the vigil of the vigil

that is my birthday, casting my bones again,
a call out of air, calm, human, not house,
nor hare or phoenix, seal or hawk.

'He's gone. He's gone . . . I can't believe it.'
I couldn't believe it. It was mid-August.
A rainbow drew a halo across the east

from bay to grassy promontory.
The Twelve Bens faced me
under the rainbow. My birthday.

The rainbow was a house for my birthday.
In this quick lodging I made my wish,
against another sad year, I meant, for her.

Evening came and faded our house.
What could I change for you? I have only
the age old jewels for a daughter

which are: passion, ruby, understanding, garnets,
courage, diamonds; and pearls. What are the pearls?
Not sorrow − you've enough −

But what Persephone might have of Demeter,
her clumsy constancy of good faith,
But not to see me, in your pain and pride

perhaps never, too late for that between us,
when I held you in my arms and you,
my serious Pierrette in blue lycra,

followed my hand as I showed you the jugs
and the svelte figurines I had lately collected
and your solemn peekaboo eyes

inspected each to learn why they were good.
I can't remember that house any more,
and the wild man, or your err man,

or mine, is stashed maybe forever in store
and my hearth can't be cooked on.

❦

Here I am, at last. We hopped, my own love

and I, across the sandbagged sea.
Nothing, after all, could hold back
either water or the long return flight, and here

where the gold moon is perfectly full
in the lavender sky to the east,
under the tucked arm of the palm-tree,

where moths flit on the vine
before the moon, here, where the hawks
crisscross their svelte evening hunt

and prance their claws at each other
in mid air and scream and silently pass on,
I sit for the time being in this island fall

and wait, not really for her call,
or for the changes that will come.

Spring–Autumn 1999

RIFF

I fell asleep on the banks of the city.
I twitched my toes in the brown mouth of the old man.
There was a boy behind me, down and out and drunk,

curled up sleeping, only his soles bare,
and the Mississippi below, lapping the baulks
of the big steps, and behind us, slow and

studying, bent to the brown notes, a tenor sax
on the boardwalk, collecting money in his cap,
melody after melody against the sky of the levee.

My absurd American dear, you began to sing away
but more tunefully than you'd ever thought
and then even I, playing along, sang friends

with the momentary marriage, when it seemed,
I thought, you thought, it could never really be,
three or four last, lapping notes, and the calm.

Santa Fé, winter

In the draught from the door
the scarlet rug flapped sharply,

a flame detached itself,
poising like a dancer,

the grand jeté
for some minutes over the San Pedros.

Day cried through my mouth,
a woman over an unlit log.

The door opened,
the rug pirouetted and glimmered.

WAYS TO GO

Having gone to the Navajos,
having waited for a great turquoise truck,
we are the forty white gazers, with forty black cameras,
bounding in ten rows of white patio chairs,
along the bed of the river,
and the guide in a felt hat, up front in the cab

A catlike sea,
      laying claim to eyes and life
            runs to the water meadows

A tray of folk chunting and ricochetting
with lopsided heaves up and down
the mud banks of old waters and new

Seasons floating out like tresses against the blunt tyres,
the whole river-hair dividing round islands
where holy beings have built aged farms,
where on wafer land ponies and foals graze
– a weak, soft muzzle nosing nine hundred feet
of water-headdressed, dark-beaded,
unsailing cloud of gold stone –

A sea runs
      to the light green water meadows

The hands of the foreign observers
weakly scatter in the water like legs, let down

Sea, laying
      claws to eyes and life,
          sidling to the mouth

The waterbug on the storm pattern rug,
whose black joints cover immensities,
over and under the water-sheet
jogs upside down under the overhang of other dimensions,

and a warm and pink cat's mouth of stone
drops each lot of forty, like kittens,
back at the beginning.

❦

The dream has brought
                    the valour of dreams
to the greenest water meadows

a catlike sea, laying
                    claim to eyes and life

padding into the mouth of the next year
                    of the same immense canyon
succinctly
                    under the blue of a moon

Not sea, breaking high and red over Utah,
washboard of faults and stresses
you and I can pound and pound at,
trying to clean. We can wipe nothing,
remember nothing, as if under a spell,
people trapped in a width of rock.

A crocodile from the Middle Ages
doubled and folded as if tortured,
as if compressed by its blood-red skin.

We're sorry, we straighten our clothing,
smoothe each other's soft hair –
that ancient caress, we soothed ourselves
in the other. And,
you bought me a pair of silver earrings,
emblem of corn and clouds and rain.

Predictable results to an extent
of the unimaginable compressive forces –
We are fascinated by the earth's snores,
the deduced twitching and bellowing
of the gut as it roils
beneath the soreness and redness of the hide.

Through two casual domes,
two mountainous loaves risen in sunlight,
between them a spired castle
set on a gleaming elevation
ten miles to the south.
A tale of the hungry man who ate

without stopping for three days
a hundred white loaves, his lanky
legs in yellow stockings laid out
among the mountains of bread, his mouth
going full blast, his delighted eye.
His tongue swiped out grottoes

and caves, a saliva burst in an hour!
And there are such grottoes –
handpainted by that which on earth
pursues the severity required
of pink, ochre, cream, terracotta, gold
and the like. The flood tongue

thrusts back into these pitchers,
ferocious and occasional.
Love, today they're dried out.
The cream slick rock capping the red cliffs
lies struck, lies robed
by the heavy white of sunlight

and brooched by piñon and flowers.
When we arrive so high – tired out,
climbing those dry folds –
then they extend to us
their ancient, desirous,
and tenderly satisfying shadows.

GOLDENTOWN

Who will remember the town
when it was blue, and green,
when it was brown and grey,
marble and stone and brick?

I stay in a blue-green township
where country churches lift up white wood spires,
silent among heavy cicadas and crickets
and endless cries of jays and crows in the woods.

Then on an evening of Glorias and Agnus Deis,
I sat on my seat, and the chorus,
as they do, lifted me out of some sorrows.
What sorrow in their light of day?

We drove west through deepening night
to our room on the Hudson, and thought
of nothing but bed and sleep and moths.
Today the unknown town burst

into its sheet of gold, in the old man's voice –
bronchial, his throat a little soupy,
but a straightforward response, report of
his inmost photography, a highlight

not quavering, though fifty-four years past.
Flights of the old pilot
soar again in the cache of colour
footage. 'Yes sir, it's true to what I saw.

I dropped what's called napalm
on an ammo train and the whole town
became golden, it just lifted up.'
The new museum of film opens.

Earlier today two US embassies
'went up in flames', in Africa,
bombed. The ensuing screams
of trapped shoppers and workers cannot

at all shake the still of memory –
the passage of the golden town that flew away.
The old man says his say.
Leaving these Glorias, walking down

into the houses of blue and green woods
and loneliness in the jay's cries,
O sad Jerusalem, how
plain to see, in black and white.

In a boudoir of mirrors
we saw multiple civic happenings.
In the hot handle
of a May New York heatwave
we saw three cocks a'crowing,
five breasts a'sailing, twenty nipples dashing
and hundreds and thousands of Os.
Seventy-nine thousands were little setsumas
jiggling on the boardwalk at Coney Island
and the mega wiggle of the balance
was a fast golden apple, juggling
down Myrtle Avenue
by hand to hand throwing
to a man dressed all in dusty green O
his head grinning under his arm,
in perfect confidence,
and a tongue quivering with a fork in it,
rippling through the silver of the screens
you had fixed
for our delectation and delight.
Do you remember? Oh you do,
whatever you say now
a million years into the frosty bite.
Here is a follow up for ten:
Have you dwindled to a cold in the head?
In those screens – it could even be
fulsome to praise the many gleaming civic events.
I feel at least able to record
it was a hundred and twenty-two in the shade
of a thousand and one afternoons
in Brooklyn, in 1984.

HOME

There's no need for sorrow
though sorrow holds my throat
like a man who comes up
to strangle me casually in a street.

There's no need to miss home
though a dense lily flowered
– on its raised leaf a frog sprawled
on the pond, under golden eyelids.

There's no need for the poem
though only frogs are at home
and you and I have systematically flown
to diametrically opposite lands.

My hand must protect my throat
in the faraway street.
Love, dear one, your hand I'd kiss
and I'd hold onto it tightly.

Jinxiang Hotel

Long plump Mandarin ducks
sculling a green moat from dawn to dusk,
uttering echoing quacks in the damp.

If you were encircled by beauty
from dawn to dusk, illimitable freeways,
glass portals entered between lions,

their nostril innards painted blue and red,
a great modern wall would contract slowly,
marching concrete inwards.

Silken thrushes, washstands, bridal beds,
bath mugs, lacquered seats, thrones,
the throne where the Emperor extended
his ten prized toenails to be trimmed,
the Hall of Supreme Harmony,
fortunes of air and fire,
– the Empress a green and blue watered earth
after the golds of defence, taxation,
reception of envoys, performance of god.

A steel lotus flower backstairs,
Cixi was the last great power.
In here Yin and Yang make a beautiful theory.
From prostituted courtesan to Dragon.
Scarlet and gold. I had
lain sweating, that weird week, in a concrete
high-rise hotel bedroom and now
only the last day found access
under windy skies
to these halls of mainly closed questions,
striding in freed, befuddled,
into blue skies, out of tunnels
through heaven's monstrous red gate.

In the Forbidden City
nothing but lichen and standing grasses
waved on the heavy roof tiles;
the bronze lion was repeated
everywhere, his duplicated claws
clamping the world. After my brilliant
plan for that year, lost out
to an absurd slumping
of corridors and bathrooms,
sickness, homesick telephone calls,

operators with fluting uncomprehending
repetitive walls of polite
intention to be helpful.
Lost – nothing could be done now.

Magic animals trooped
down the golden green gables
to draw off the lightning,
a nobleman riding a pig each time led
the small silhouetted cavalcades downhill.
I explored the streets all day,
artists, concubines, officials, maids,
behind hill-like walls.
I and other people all day
were absorbed through halls,
one to the next,
like a bland fluid drawn
through many layers of dusty muslin.

Open to north, south, east, west
under kite-soaring skies.
Not now the conductor of harm.
The ins and outs have changed.
On the outside,
in the long plains of Tian'anmen Square,
the running children loop their kites,
a conversation wide and high above me.
Tired on a balmy, summery
evening in China, I watch them
repeating, twirling, rocking –
What goes up must one day,
it always has, however slowly,
topple to the wind.

SONG OF THE BULLDOZERS

In memory,
Jenin Camp, the West Bank, 04.02

We are the diggers of Jenin,
we dig and then we bury things.

Like sofas, fridges, golden rings,
terrorists and little girls.

See how the wicked cripple hurls
himself before us down the drains,

and how we take enormous pains
to reach through walls for dads and mums,

compacting them to kingdom come
or Paradise if they insist,

and ten to one they can't resist.
How sweet the body parts do sleep,

beneath the quiet of Jenin streets.
So breathe now, breathe, in Tel Aviv,

where bulldozers have come to live.

He lights on the singing post.
He makes the most
of the frilled embers
of the sun.

There's a locker room
of sparrows, until in one
dancing team they whirl
to the stream.

He ignores the plodding
of my boots, and a single car
swallowing the boots
in its din.

But round he twists,
body bouncing on the post,
and tracking what I think
I hear, can't see

and never do, the other.
Way along the lane,
a wire of song.
My robin sings.

THE BUTTERFLY

I said to her facetiously,
I am hunting the heraldic butterfly
of fame and love and
of not seeing my child's ghost
rejected at every party turn.

But she said,
that's the heraldic insect of heaven
who only descends
to flutter on the foreheads
of those already in ghosthood.

Then I anxiously said,
this butterfly flutters onto the face
down a lane hung with panniers of iced plums.
The angels write of it:
over the top but they write.

Then I enviously went on,
I see foreheads around me
cursed with that scarab's claw,
inviolate, blessed
with all the fruits of the world.

But she said, pursing her lips,
isn't it a cliché,
and no smoke without fire,
that in the middle of the night
your fruit figures,

they too must twist and turn,
peeled by some twist
of their mother's indifference,
her waist, her hands, her figured breasts,
and not all the sweetest flesh . . .

Running and running down that void avenue
. . . see how the trees wave,
the large-eyed shadow flicks, here, there,
zig-zags towards you,
scribbles written by angels across its wings.

Two fritillaries twit across the tall thistles
in the cowfield, where the cows decently
absent themselves, basking behind great boulders,
so that I'm not scared.
                    In the fog, planes bat
boulders together like thunder, but I'm
a Mrs Gulliver tied happily in grasses I asked for.
Flies bat their own boulders across my face,
whatever those could be,
                    tangles and knots in
the yarn of the fog wrapping my grasses.
The two butterflies are as dodgy and flirty
as teenagers, and the larger darker ones
lollop along
            among the lower herbs.
I've reached not Lilliput but somewhere,
the coast of a woolly white future
where not just the land but also the sea,
air, everything from
                    now on is drowned.
Desire lies in the land of the steamy pasture
as pleased with butterflies and stones as
the heifers beyond the boulders. Lyonesse
gained, or laziness . . .
                    A true name
should be kept under the dark books
of indolent standing stones and sat upon,
and no one allowed to lift them.
Lifted, the air
            will fall open
and a dun land and sea reread itself.
Today is Sunday. Let Lyonesse of the blessed
stay wrecked. I never pray; I keep asking

bells to ring out
           from under the woollen waves
for all their dead saints. Being as cold
as an imagined saint. Butterflies, they say,
flirt like the light finger of future,
like gloves I'll put on
           for warmth one day
and needing my warmth. Grasses and
roaming butterflies: a field where each boulder
turned out of place might be its sister boulder,
or glove, or spidery yarn, or
                mist.

RENVYLE

To live out a long fate.
To wave it in like a boat bringing the mail.
An owl cries on Tully Mountain
across the throat of a sea
as silvered as my old hand mirror.

Beyond, there lies Renvyle,
and the hotel we winkled out;
it had vanished for seventy years.
Where my grey-eyed young mother
and my curly-haired young Dada to be

lay under this same half Edam moon.
For a marriage gift they could see
a slip of Sligo, and Mayo,
and half of Connemara the beautiful.
In a big brown register

they wrote their inky names, hers
become his, precarious, not so black,
though her 'Elizabeth' is inked firm,
and not, then, shaky, infirm.
Sometimes now, it quavers, the whole

name, as the half shied at that page.
'And did you get to Renvyle?'
on our return. 'The first time I ever
signed it': exaggerating, charmed,
– her voice strong as her life's hand.

The owl on the mountain cries twice,
the sun heads for the sea
like a red bull for its black barn of cloud.
The sheep cry on the gentle hill.
Over Ballynakill Bay a dog echoes.

Those Twelve Bens bend down so low,
my own name, carrying hers inside,
shakes in the mirror, a hand
into the dark sea, cold to my throat . . .
How I swam in the rare sun, this morning!

The prince in his sleep

I sat by you all day,
a most unfamiliar behaviour,
you deep asleep, the sleeping prince
returned to his beauty, my mother
would have said. Love in the mist,
poor thing, she could hardly see you.

Sometimes she stood and bent and kissed
your narrowing forehead and
called out loudly in her strong
deaf voice, 'My darling, I want to
keep you but I think God may want you.'
You narrowed and sank all day.

I saw your golden eyelids,
fragile, unwritten speech, smooth
as they hadn't been – Remembering
the months and years of a sad haste . . .
Ten seconds to spare, you'd open
your blue eyes lazily and wide,

your blue eyes, good as a good child,
shy, sly at your chosen curious day,
your deeds; proud, modest. The space
of your life was wide. I rattled, fell
into your space regularly, but
we, or you, or I, smoothed out,

filled in, planted a sprig, a flag,
departed smiling. It never stopped,
your switchback and my small career
colliding and keeping up, laughing,
sometimes besides myself. Your eyelids,
closed, transparent, authoritative.

. . . Transparent, authoritative.
I could laugh at your leg pulls
for what they were worth, but
afterwards. At the time I couldn't cope.

All day I held one of your hands.
Your left hand. Did that signify?
I was lucky. There were so many
who wanted your stilled, big hands.

Long, squared, fleshy fingers, thumb.
I'd never thought such rough tough hands
were shapely. (My mother would kiss your hand
and back you'd tenderly kiss her hand.)

You grew more golden in the low
barred light. The room was designed
for low voices, for any extremes, for us,
for your dying. The act of.

I understood your act. I was part of it.
'But can you understand, I'm a man of action.'
This act was undertaken in slow and
contracting breaths, the flame going back

to the wick. By the undreaming end,
the throat only the site of breath. The breath
hovered for a while in the lowest crease
of your old throat, there, not there,

there . . . not there. Only the wick. Holding
your long hand, utterly still, the man
who couldn't keep still. Not there.
Whatever that was to mean in later days.

THE WATCH

He would take his left wrist
by his right hand, stooping down
over his watch to squint out the figures.

Was it time? Was it near to the news?
or to dinner? to six? or to eight?
He was a hawk of misty time.

A tall flower grows by the door.
My mother carries the watch on her arm,
and she sits in the same wistful house.

He sits by the open door: 'Who's there?'
Catching my flypast: 'The headlines will do.'
And now, what am I waiting for?

I can bear your absence now,
a weight like an avalanche on
a village, that never falls,
or the way the glacier is glued
to a million rock faces, and that
tonnes of blue ice hang vertical
like a coat on a hook for all time.

A man comes out of the glacier
where the icy torrents scatter
down the granite moraine,
a man in a suit and a tie
that's keeping his trousers up,
and his feet in tennis shoes
as worn yellow as the tail of ice.

Dot

Twelve months ago, little yellow man,
king of the golden river, I laid you out
on your white deathbed, with no difficulty.

Months on, little old man in a fairytale,
join your hands, your nose, chin,
eyes, dots dancing timidly.

A silver satin butterfly considers my
finger, the pungency of my skin, in sun
by the rim of the sweeping precipice

where pink campion and bellflowers
of the purple upland line the perilous
pathway to the glass pinnacled seracs.

Only a dot, a rock, a speckle of grit,
old king, laid under the buckled mirrors,
no eye, nose, mouth, nothing to be seen.

When the seagulls scream around the house
    at half past five
and the two collared doves sit cooing or cawing
    on the telephone pole
    plumped comfortably
not far from my window, on the minuscule peak,

then I think of the souls of the dear and the departed,
    of yours in fact,
since I believe in no other; and of the bodies
    of those living uneasily,
    waking at this hour;
you without body, nor any seagull, to be
    haunting the chimney,

or myself your daughter whose body and mind
    altogether remember you,
though all I have not seen is the place of your ashes:
    under the willow-tree
    by the Thames, that flowed
by other banks in your ceaseless years in their long days.

The kind man laid what was
left of you in a trail that he sprang
like breadcrumbs out of a golden bucket
round and round a weeping willow-tree.

I don't know if robins and forest birds
flew off with them, or ravens or vultures,
but of course they had gone, ashes to
earth, long before I got there,

long before his gardener showed me,
crudely. Other dads' floral tributes,
lilies, finished or flowering, inserted by the pot,
a wrinkle of old marigolds; they were there.

'So are there others?' 'Lots of people,'
he said, turning back, 'lots of people.'
I sat on the hard lawn and couldn't retrace
my path or self to this

in Mortlake, under a green canopy
propped with crumbled lilies
and sweet, irrelevant, tacky cards.
I took a photo. The river path was well

behind the iron railings. I'd thought
he might be special, on his own, at
least his burned old bones. I'd thought
he'd be nearer the river, that flows

past the flat in Chelsea, and Parliament
of course. Had he loved the river?
Sports he loved. Up in the long-fingered
twigs some other son or daughter had slung

some other father's FC badge
on a blue ribbon, and a little chime hung
among the leaves, and other little things
he might have liked. How unlike

us in our disdain for one another, or
anything of that sort, our terrible
turning away from all that might be
love, memory, an ordinary wisdom.

Tell me, how can the spreading circles
be broken, of the dust, the empty lawns,
the railing? How can this one clipped tree
be part of the wood, or bend itself to the river?

ANNIVERSARY

I put right what wasn't right
or seemed not right, not seemly
though you can never know,
you in thin air now or truer, in thick earth.

Someone trailed your bones
in a sad place, under a weeping willow,
not even yours alone, a mass burial,
a shared plot. A plot not shared,

truer to say. I lost your last
act of death, and was sad, it seemed
no honour, unseemly. Now I've
sown the seams of your earth,

committed you after the act,
sent you a bunch of ten red roses.
A good man who never knew you
laid them by the tree, sent a picture

unasked. The last act,
another act of your death:
to let my mother know, through
her silence. Her pleasure, her surprise.

When you were with me in the world
we inhabited, the only one,
it seemed I had all the time
to muse on my father's flight out,
a tough old ball kicked out of touch
in a moment. With you still
there, I'd have time to catch the speed
of my father's throw, his people,
his work, his talk, bright-eyed,
impatient, charmer repentant, self on the go.

To say you've gone. You too?
The two who were one because
always the two. What do I say
now, of his death: that it propped you
in astonished, blinded anguish.
How you said after, you 'chose to live',
that you had your own 'mission',
to see, to help, what would become
of us, our children, how live,
how flourish, how you could help.

Poor mother, how could you help
each day multiplying into sleep,
your good sense, even your fatwa –
the book, the book, it has to be written!
You like a little animal hunched
dozing on the old yellow sofa,
but glad always to charm the guest,
the guest of your house, welcomed
with the open smile of decades.
Then my father, dreamed of,
a frightening ghost, desperado ghost,
for where so sadly did he wander,

in forgotten hospital corridors, forgotten,
and how could you help him?

The last August, our birthdays, both –
you sat down, hunched,
our Mrs Tiggiwinkle, on the bed
I'd christened your daybed, where
between tall windows you slept
the summer afternoons, your garden green.
One morning, such stiff pain from
upstairs bed to downstairs bed, you
slowly sat, without looking at me:
'What's it for?' All you could say.
A year on, facing no hope, no death.

I couldn't bear to know.
What you'd always feared, and I
also, the unuseful quiet: the void.
Never in both your two lives
did you let that sneaky void,
that snag in the good gardener's working
day, that small wizened worm,
the bite at the end of the world,
get you. I hastily talked. You turned,
lay down, finished the painful
movement, without comment.

By the wall

You stood by the corner of the house:
your magnolia not yet the altar of the chalices
of the creamy spring.

When all was cold, you stood by the wall.
Your voice became reedy; it was the one last straw
that spanned the gulf,

the void-sucking gulf; that stemmed
the dew in the leaves of the leafless tulip-tree
that held up the wall

that held up the house that held up the room
where you would come to the half-tenanted bed,
in that after-life.

In the bronze autumn, before the rain,
I came to scatter your ashes, over the green grass,
the yew, the heather.

I stood in the last still day, where your rumple-
trunked tulip-tree held up its yellow mourning hands
and let them fall.

JUST AFTER MIDNIGHT

23.10.02

Just after midnight long time gone
you set aside your slipper
onto the step of the house
and as you came into
the house, barefoot left it.

You would talk of your sleeping prince,
waking him with that kiss,
such whims in the garden maze,
a modern woman's pounce.
I walked in the sun of your walk.

Our tales hang by their cherry ribbons.
Silks and satins, cotton, rag.
How all the dazzlers danced
for you. How midnight
carried you off, brightest moon.

LAVENDER

Those are the weeks I talk to you
as though you are still my mother,
my lavender sachet tied with a blue silk ribbon

keeping my summer dresses and yours.
As if the little lavender sachet mother
tied with silk, as they used to long ago,

could tell me what to wear and cry out
'Courage!' in French, who ever knew why,
on a tough rising, as you used to.

Now you are gone to earth,
by myself tilled into your own pleasures,
your roses, your pines, your clematis,

where you wrote and read and took notes
and, pretending not, lately you dozed.
If you are merely me now?

You in me? We're no double act,
no holy mother mystery. Who am I
inside my clothes? The ashes

of a child's mother's fragrance?

BEFORE CHRISTMAS

One smile tilted at your lips
under the landslide of sleep.

You closed your blind, dark blue eyes.
Against me or the light?

The past is always, only here,
just before dead Christmas.

'Her body shutting down.' I understood.
(Like a factory, a company?)

'Everything packing up.'
One who moves house and goes away.

Your blood thin hands, your bone thin arms
slapping against the pillow.

Then, your calm,
O irrevocable sculpture.

Deep into the wild rose flowers
I see the young beauty, severe white-haired,

the girl in her satin wedding,
the dark-haired writer's indrawn gaze,

then, and then. Tonight
is the shut bedroom, and the moment

of birth, even, for look how you leaned back
against pillows, far away,

how you unsqueezed your eyes
to inspect your latest 'little creature',

and how did I look to you?
I must have turned and wobbled

with blind eyes, mouth, seeking
your breast, your eyes; but now, tonight, where

is the fair smile nourishing, hungered for?

My brave sister

for Jane

All the parents are dead,
though all the children thought
they'd live forever.
The room is warm and bright,

and nests its mute and
sleeping mistress like a swan.
You and my 'revolutionary sister'
chat in the eiderdown!

Did you dream for me,
two kisses to this hurting?
What I hadn't had, by the wretch
of chance: her departing?

Dear, how I wish,
on these sunlit afternoons
where she'll not sit and lift
her face to the sun again,

you and my brave sister
(years dead in a fast car)
could loll and smoothe on the sun
where her joints are sore,

and heap her fine stories
among the plumped pillows.
We are left in these kind hangings,
with no mothers.

I will christen your dream:
of us two first and here:
and of a gauze of figures
in a bed that filled a bower:

but, in my ear,
as dear a voice, or tone,
as the small birds that go quiet
after the dawn.

THE FRIGATE-BIRD

The aeronautic frigate-bird
– you never saw that –
chancing its great wings high up
over the shining half-water-buried
fish in the bay. These ikons
of the near sky – oh I last dreamt of flying
years and years ago.

Who knows your dreams,
what do they count, now? I spread out
your ashes over bush and flower,
round plum and apple tree,
in magic circles not thought of
in the long-shadowed planted days.

Everyone's mother is an ikon.
Nobody knows that until she's failing,
falling into the sea.
How can I think of her here
– bay, ocean, unknown to her –
where the bright tropics snatch up
all decay, all mists?

She could have liked
to sit here, see what I see, sit here,
palms, parasols, pelicans!
Whatever would please you –
How can I circle you
with what would have pleased you?

How with closed eyes
death's castle lies nearly open to you.
What will you find there, the ogre
we all fear or your particular love,
your old classic of the sleeping prince
who would have kissed you
if he could, but was too asleep.
I hope this pretty meeting will be
yours again, is yours now.

The Saturday before you died
I moved inadvertently
between your closed eyes and the light,
and your blind blue eyes shot wide
open. You opened your eyes
often, like that; it could
have been distress or dream.
I leaned down quickly,
calling, 'Mummy, it's Judith, Judith,'
as loud as I dared, in case.

You smiled, your lips twisted
for one moment, the effort
the stroke had squeezed you to,
you of the lionhearted smile.
A year or more before, shocked, blunt,
I'd asked, 'Have you forgotten how
to smile?' At which, willing, you'd tried
a mask of a grin, the first for weeks.

I cheered it on and, heaven knows,
you could take any useful hint. Slowly
you smiled a way back to your lips,
your stiffened cheeks. Little half smile,

excalibur of a smile, risen towards light
from the drown of body and mind.
Perhaps my misted call. You closed
your eyes. Your face, my mother,
forever gone behind the light,
into the castle. I kiss you, and one
for my father, for each of the two;
but each one sleeps.